RUNES for: *Divination* (Basic)

Books by R. Briski

RUNES for: *Divination* (Basic)

(Coming Soon)
RUNES for: *Divination* (Advanced)

RUNES for:
Divination (Basic)

Runes: the ancient and mysterious symbols of a forgotten age.

By

R. Briski

Copyright © 2010 R. Briski

All Rights Reserved. No part of this publication may be reproduced in any form or by any means, electronic or mechanical, including photocopying, scanning, recording or by any information storage and retrieval system, without permission in writing from the author.

Brief quotations for reviews and articles about the publication are authorized.

ISBN: 978-0-9827921-0-0

Printed in the United States of America

This book is dedicated to
my ancestors.

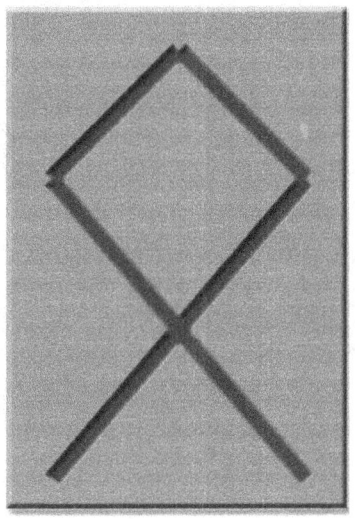

OTHALA

*Awaken the Slumbering Dragon
of Ancestral Might*

And of course to my wife Astara, without whom, none of this would have been possible.

Table of Contents

Preamble 1
Source.. 2
Origin of the Runes 2
Brief History.................................... 5
Usage 7
Talismans & Symbols 10
Divination 14
The 3 Aettir 17
Runes and their Meanings............ 19
Freyja's Aett 20
FEHU 22
URUZ 24
THURISAZ..................................... 26
ANSUZ 28
RAIDHO 30
KENAZ 32
GEBO... 34
WUNJO 36
Heimdall's Aett 38
HAGALAZ..................................... 40
NAUTHIZ...................................... 42
ISA 44
JERA 46
EIHWAZ 48
PERTHRO...................................... 50
ELHAZ.. 52
SOWILO 54

Tiwaz's Aett 56
TIWAZ 58
BERKANO 60
EHWAZ 62
MANNAZ 64
LAGUZ 66
INGWAZ 68
DAGAZ 70
OTHALA 72
Rune Readings 74
The Three Rune Spread 76
Example #1: 78
Example #2: 82
The Nine Rune Spread 84
Runic Interrelationships 86
Rune Tines 88
Runes, Tarot & Astrology 90
Thank You 93

Preamble

In this book I will focus on the usage of the Runes for Divination purposes. The use of Runes and Runic symbols for talismans I will leave for another time.

Further, this book is meant to be more of a beginners guide to using the Runes for divination purposes, as such, detailed lore about the Runes and more complex divination practices and methods will also be saved for another volume.

However, having said that, even an experienced Runster will find beneficial information and perhaps a new way of looking at the Runes.

Rory Briski

Source

The word Rune comes from several ancient Germanic dialects and historically has meant "secret" or "mystery". The word root also has a vocal meaning of "whisper" or "roar". Therefore each Rune can be thought of as an individual unit of secret knowledge. So that each Rune or unit represents a unique mystery or principal of arcane lore.

Origin of the Runes

It is through the Norse God of Magic, Odhin, that gods and men are able to receive the wisdom of the Runes.

Odhin was the first being to be initiated into the Runic mysteries by extracting the Rune wisdom directly from the source, and it infused into his being.

RUNES for: *Divination (Basic)*

When the essence of the Runic knowledge merged within him, he was able to formulate the means to communicate their nature to other beings.

The shamanistic like initiation of Odhin upon the tree Yggdrasill is interpreted from the Poedic Edda, The Saying of Hár: "Hávamál", stanzas 138 and 139:

> I know that I hung
> on the wind-tossed tree
> all of nights nine,
> wounded by spear
> and given to Odhin;
> myself to myself,
> on that tree,
> which no man knows,
> from what roots it does rise.
>
> Neither drink nor bread
> they gave me,

Rory Briski

I looked below me,
I picked up the runes
I took them screaming,
I fell back to the ground.

RUNES for: *Divination (Basic)*

Brief History

The oldest Runic system, the 24 stave Elder Futhark, dates back to at least 200BCE. This set of ideographs was used extensively until around 800CE. Around this time, 800CE, the Elder Futhark was slowly transformed into the Younger Futhark consisting of only 16 Runes. Also during the time of the Elder Futhark an Anglo-Saxon derivative was developed that contained 28 Rune-staves.

These sets and several other types of Runic systems have been developed over the years but none have matched the pureness of form of the Elder Futhark.

Some books on Runes have also changed the original order of the runes, why this was done is open to conjecture, but I for one reject these random rearrangements.

Rory Briski

For one, the name of the runes, "Futhark", is actually an acronym of the first six runes of the set: **F**ehu, **U**ruz, **Th**urisaz, **A**nsuz, **R**aidho & **K**enaz.

Further, the runes are in the order they are in not by whim of chance, but due to their specific meanings and how they relate to one another.

This book uses the original 24 Rune-staves, in their original order.

RUNES for: *Divination (Basic)*

Usage

Initially, the Runes were used singularly, as a pictograph or glyph, to represent some specific magical concept. As time progressed, the Runes were developed into an alphabet, but their magical significance was never lost. And eventually the Runes were combined into composite images to hold a higher esoteric meaning. Used as house marks or personal seals, they augmented coat-of-arms and heraldic symbols.

Their usage can even be seen today in some parts of the USA and Western Europe by the practice of putting a horse-shoe above a door for good health. The shape of a horse-shoe is basically that of the rune Uruz. A rune of Healing, Vital Strength and Homeland.

Rory Briski

The two most common uses of the Runes were for divination and as talismans. As talismans they were routinely used to provide good luck, protection and offensive power.

When studying the Runes, each Rune is interpreted in a slightly different manner depending on if it appears in a casting of lots for divination purposes, or if it is inscribed on an item as a talisman.

RUNES for: *Divination (Basic)*

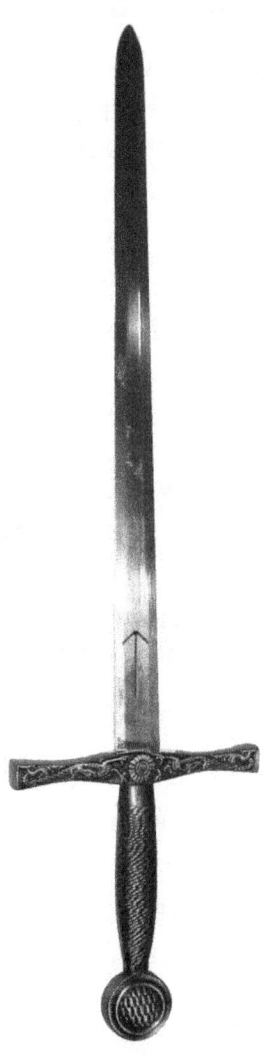

A sword with the Rune Tiwaz near the hilt, for victory and justice.

Rory Briski

Talismans & Symbols

Used singularly, a Runic symbol has a great deal of force and power in and of itself. Historically, they are said to bring the wearer wisdom, wealth and luck. They were also used to offer protection from enemies and fears, or to give the wearer the strength to overcome them.

Talismans and symbols were carved on everything from wood to metal and from stone to bone. Swords inscribed with Runic symbols are common, as are bracelets and necklaces.

Several Runes used together, as in a bind Rune, provides an amplified power base. However, a great deal of care must be taken when creating bind Runes, a misdrawn composite could spell disaster for the Rune carver.

Many early graves had Runes carved into their stones. However, the most prolific medium was wood and bone.

RUNES for: *Divination (Basic)*

Both being easy materials to obtain and easy to work with. They also had the added bonus of once containing a life force.

Unfortunately, the ravages of time took its toll on the runes made of wood and bone. What we are left with to study are runes in stone markers and metal items. Yet occasionally, we see them in the wooden frames of building structures, in older places in Iceland, where the manufacture of home design is practiced in similar fashion to how it was done many centuries ago.

For example, the framing in some buildings shows clear runic patterns and yet serve no structural purpose. They build them that way because their fathers, grandfathers and great grandfathers built them that way. And so some of the lore is preserved, even if they do not now recognize it as such.

Rory Briski

The above is an example of a Talisman (Bind Rune) that I created for a non-profit organization. It was created with the following three Runes.

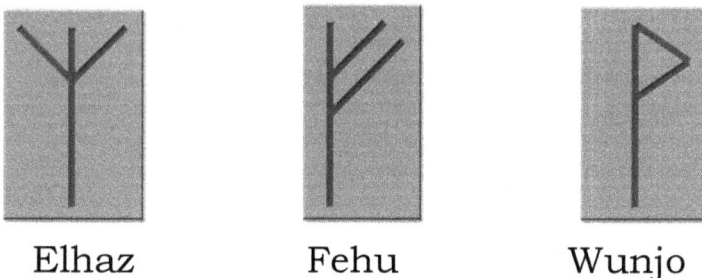

Elhaz   Fehu   Wunjo

ELHAZ: Communication Between Self & Higher Self, Spiritual Growth, Divine Communication and Cleansing & Warding

RUNES for: *Divination (Basic)*

FEHU: Magical Force, Mobile Wealth (Money, Jewelry) & Using Wealth (Money and Knowledge) Wisely and Generously

WUNJO: Self-Confidence in an Integrated Personality, Emotional and Physical Healing, Social and Domestic Harmony, Ideal Harmonization, Cope with or Elimination of Pain and New Social Relationships

BIND RUNE MEANING

Divinely protected and attaining the inner guidance, insight and wisdom to attract wealth and knowledge, in order to use it wisely and generously, to create emotional & physical healing and social & domestic harmony.

Rory Briski

Divination

Traditionally, runecasting is a true act of direct communication between humans and the divinities of the many realms. The runecasters' will, ability, knowledge, level of being and understanding are all very important in interpreting how the Runes relate to the present situation.

When the Runes are thrown onto a table or drawn from a bag, it is thought that certain entities manipulate the Runes so they fall or are drawn out in a particular way. These forces could be manifest from the Great Norns: Urdhr, Verhandi and Skuld; or from other entities such as valkyries or the runesters' guides.

The oldest known method of divination was to cast the Runes onto the ground and without looking to draw three of

RUNES for: *Divination (Basic)*

them. The order in which the Runes are drawn is very important.

The Runes as they relate to the three Norns are:

➢ The first relates to Urdhr: That which has become (the past),

➢ The second relates to Verhandi: That which is becoming (roughly the present),

➢ The third represents Skuld: That which may come to pass given past events (the future).

Runecasting is not so much an attempt to predict future events, but a way of attuning yourself to the web of interlocking <u>potential</u> futures that are woven all around us.

The most likely future course or event may become clear, based on what has transpired in the past, if no other

Rory Briski

course of action is undertaken to change it.

The ancients considered the future to always be in motion, and the future was shaped by past events. Remember, the present is only here for a fleeting moment, we are always moving into the future from an ever growing past.

RUNES for: *Divination (Basic)*

The 3 Aettir

The Elder Futhark is divided into three groups of eight Runes each. These groups are called aettir.

Each set of eight runes, derive their group name, or aett name, from the god/goddess that holds sway over the first rune of that set.

The first eight runes are called Freyja's aett, for the Goddess Freyja. Freyja is a goddess associated with love, beauty, fertility, gold, magic, war and death. This aett symbolizes the creation of the cosmos, order out of chaos and creation.

The second eight runes are called Heimdall's aett. Heimdall guards the Bifrost bridge which connects Midgard (Earth) and Asgard (the place of gods). This aett symbolizes forces that

Rory Briski

disrupt the patterns of the first aett and can cause great change.

The last eight runes are called Tiwaz's aett after the God Tyr. Tyr is the god of law and justice as well as heroism in battle. This aett is essentially the aett of the gods and divinity.

RUNES for: *Divination (Basic)*

Runes and their Meanings

As each rune is described in the next section, you well see the following:

- The name of the aett the Rune belongs to and its position in the aett
- If there is an element (Earth, Air, Fire, Water) associated with it, not all runes have these associations
- A drawing of the Rune
- Several historical associations or meanings of the Rune (with the one in italics being the most common meaning)
- Positive/Negative aspects are listed and are consulted depending on the other aspects in the reading

Information about casting the Runes and using them for a divination reading can be found after the sections describing the Runes.

Freyja's Aett

The first aett is called Freyja's aett. It is formed of the essential elements and abilities that the runester must have developed within him or her self.

This aett is most aligned with the origins of the cosmos. Beginning with basic energy and continuing on with the ability to control, shape and use these energies:

- Magical force (fehu)
- Vital shaping power (uruz)
- Dynamic / active force (thurisaz)
- Inspiration and magic-skill (ansuz)
- Rhythm and timing (raidho)

RUNES for: *Divination (Basic)*

- Control of energies and skill to craft them (kenaz)
- The ability to give and receive power (gebo)
- Self-confidence in an integrated personality (wunjo)

Rory Briski

FEHU

Freyja's Aett: 1-1
Element: FIRE

RUNES for: *Divination (Basic)*

Conceptual Associations:
- *Mobile Wealth (Money, Jewelry)*
- Magical Force
- Raw Primal Energy
- Transfer of Energy
- Creation and Destruction
- Birth, Life, Death & Rebirth
- Fertility
- Libido
- Sexual Energy
- Using Wealth (Money and Knowledge) Wisely and Generously

Keyword Associations:
- Wealth / Poverty
- Sharing / Greed
- Excitement / Burnout

Rory Briski

URUZ

Freyja's Aett: 1-2
Element: WATER

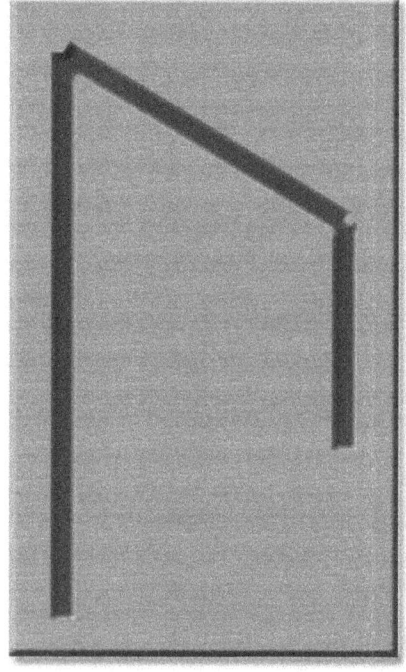

RUNES for: *Divination (Basic)*

Conceptual Associations:
    Vital Shaping Power
    Homeland
    Rune of Healing
    Vital Strength
    Organic Life Energy
    Powerful Shaping Energies

Keyword Associations:
    Strength / Weakness
    Health / Sickness
    Understanding / Ignorance
    Homeland Defense / Obsessive Possessiveness

THURISAZ

Freyja's Aett: 1-3
Element: NONE

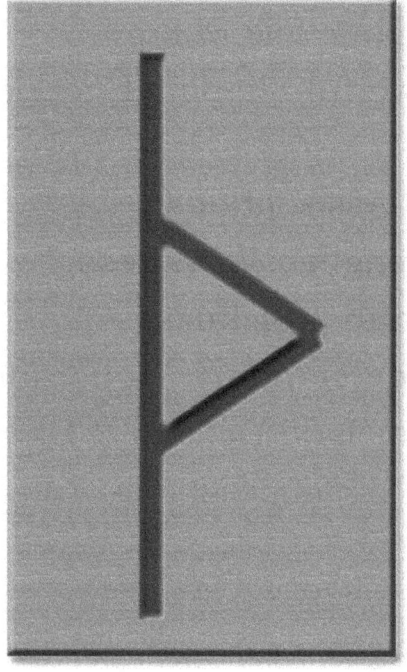

RUNES for: *Divination (Basic)*

Conceptual Associations:
- *(Aimed/Focused) Might & Melding*
- Revenge
- Mighty Warding
- Dynamic Active Force
- Danger May Be Present
- Reaction To Your Deeds May Be Dangerous
- Transformation of Force into Kinetic Energy
- Rune of Crisis and a Catalyst for Change

Keyword Associations:
- Reactive Force / Defenselessness
- Vital Eroticism / Compulsion
- Directed Force / Dullness

Rory Briski

ANSUZ

Freyja's Aett: 1-4
Element: AIR

RUNES for: *Divination (Basic)*

Conceptual Associations:
- *Creative Inspiration*
- Magic Skill
- Divine Conscious Power
- Power of Persuasion (Words)
- Responsibility to Ancestors
- Self-Transformation
- Expect the Unexpected
- Beware of Manipulation
- Bring Together Separate Elements to Understand

Keyword Associations:
- Inspiration / Misunderstanding
- Transformation / Manipulation
- Synthesis / Delusion

RAIDHO

Freyja's Aett: 1-5
Element: NONE

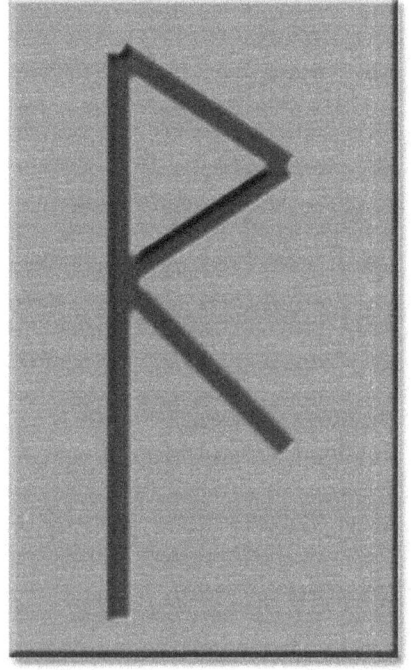

RUNES for: *Divination (Basic)*

Conceptual Associations:
- *Rhythm and Timing*
- Ordered Movement
- Ward While Traveling
- Judgment – Soul of Law
- Long Journey – Growth
- Ordered Change – Action
- "Planned" Action is Necessary
- Beware of Bad Advice

Keyword Associations:
- Rationality / Irrationality
- Action / Rigidity
- Justice / Injustice
- Ordered Growth / Stasis

Rory Briski

KENAZ

Freyja's Aett: 1-6
Element: FIRE

RUNES for: *Divination (Basic)*

Conceptual Associations:
- *Shaping Things*
- Craft of Smith
- Transformation
- Analysis (Break into Parts)
- "Fire" of Divine Inspiration
- All Works of Knowledge into Action
- Rest and Relaxation Allow Creativity to Rise
- Control of Energies and the Skills to Craft Them

Keyword Associations:
- Creativity / Lack
- Offspring / Break-up
- Ability / Inability

Rory Briski

GEBO

Freyja's Aett: 1-7
Element: NONE

RUNES for: *Divination (Basic)*

Conceptual Associations:
- *Equal Exchange of Energies*
- Love Magic
- Spend wisely
- Ability to Give and Receive Power
- Friendship, Loyalty & Hospitality
- Ritual Payment Must Be Made (Give & Take)
- May Receive a Material or Spiritual Gift
- Expect to Receive or Bestow Credit or Honor
- Synchronistic Experience
- Do NOT Depend on Gifts

Keyword Associations:
- Generosity / Influence Buying
- Honor / Greed
- Magical Exchange / Dependence

Rory Briski

WUNJO

Freyja's Aett: 1-8
Element: NONE

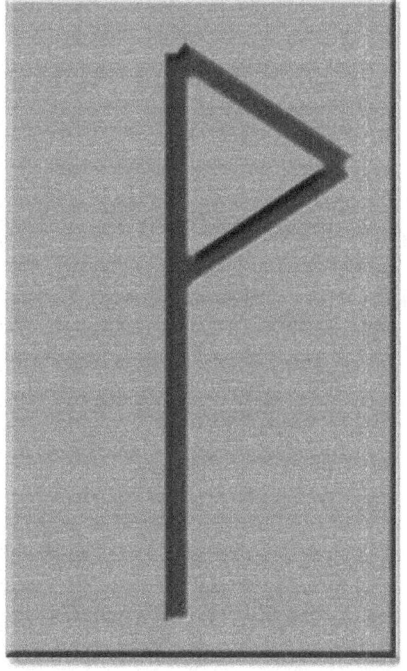

RUNES for: *Divination (Basic)*

Conceptual Associations:
> *Self-Confidence in an Integrated Personality*
> Emotional Healing
> Physical Healing
> Ideal Harmonization
> Balanced / Integrated Personality
> Social and Domestic Harmony
> Cope With or Eliminate Pain
> Strive for Ideals
> Organize Things
> New Social Relationships
> Don't Lose Your Identity to the Group

Keyword Associations:
> Harmony / Alienation
> Joy / Sorrow
> Prosperity / Strife

Rory Briski

Heimdall's Aett

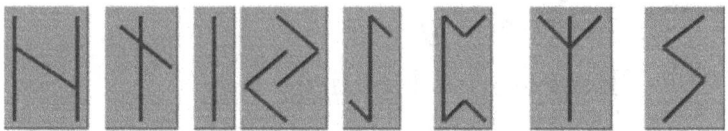

The second aett is called Heimdall's aett. It holds the Runes associated with the shape of the cosmos and the runester's initiation into higher levels of consciousness.

The energies of this aett are:

➢ The wholeness of universal structure (hagalaz)
➢ Testing to awaken the inner fire (nauthiz)
➢ Primal ice and the bridge of consciousness (isa)
➢ Cycles of the year and the growth of the seeds of power (jera)

RUNES for: *Divination (Basic)*

- The vertical trunk of Yggdrasill and the initiation by ordeal (eihwaz)
- The Well of Wyrd and the ability of the runester to use its power (perthro)
- The Bifrost bridge and the communication between the runester and their valkyrja (elhaz)
- The wheel of the sun and the runesters magical will (sowilo)

Rory Briski

HAGALAZ

Heimdall's Aett: 2-1
Element: ICE

RUNES for: *Divination (Basic)*

Conceptual Associations:

Change or Transformation of Life Structure (Crisis or Trauma)

Be Prepared for Crisis

Wholeness of Universal Structure - "Hail"

Mighty Warding Against Entropic Forces

Completion and Bringing into Being

Seed of Becoming – New Creation

Develop Pure, Crystalline Ideas and Principals

Keyword Associations:

Controlled Crisis / Crisis

Harmony / Catastrophe

Change / Stagnation

Rory Briski

NAUTHIZ

Heimdall's Aett: 2-2
Element: FIRE

RUNES for: *Divination (Basic)*

Conceptual Associations:

Strength to meet Trials and Overcome Them

The "Need" Rune

Hysterical Strength

Testing to Awaken Inner Fire

Cause and Effect

Action and Reaction

Turn Stress into Strength

Necessity is the Mother of Invention

Beware of Hostile Environment

Danger on the "Easy" Path

Unleashing of Potential Energy on All Levels – Energy Generated from Within

Keyword Associations:

Strength / Constraint

Innovation / Toil

Self-Reliance / Drudgery

Rory Briski

ISA

Heimdall's Aett: 2-3
Element: ICE

RUNES for: *Divination (Basic)*

Conceptual Associations:
- *Absolute Contraction & Stasis*
- Primal Ice
- Bridge to Consciousness
- Rune of Binding
- Stabilize Personality
- Unbreakable Will & Concentration
- Self-Control
- Unity of Purpose

Keyword Associations:
- Ego-Consciousness / Ego-Mania
- Unity / Dissipation
- Self-Control / Dullness

Rory Briski

JERA

Heimdall's Aett: 2-4
Element: EARTH

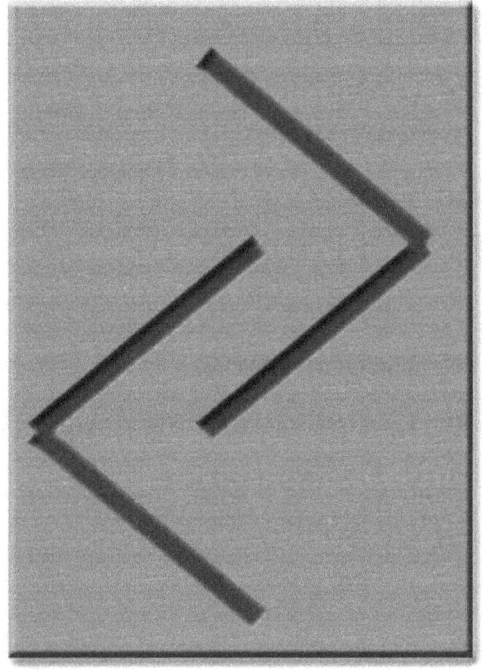

RUNES for: *Divination (Basic)*

Conceptual Associations:
> *Patience and Awareness*
> Cycles of Year
> Material Well-Being
> Growth of Seeds of Power
> Rules the Creative Process
> Long Term Planning
> Reward for Right Action
> Expect a Good Harvest
> Aid in Growth of Own Understanding
> Beware Enslavement to Repetitious Behavior

Keyword Associations:
> Plenty / Poverty
> Peace / Conflict
> Good Timing / Bad Timing

Rory Briski

EIHWAZ

Heimdall's Aett: 2-5
Element: FIRE

RUNES for: *Divination (Basic)*

Conceptual Associations:
- *Connects Above & Below*
- Initiation By Ordeal
- Connects Life & Death
- Speak with the Dead
- Initiate Controlled Changes
- Beware of Burn-Out
- The Vertical Trunk of the World-Tree Yggdrasill
- Mental Toughness and Flexibility are Needed
- Rune of Will That Survives Death & Rebirth Again & Again

Keyword Associations:
- Enlightenment / Confusion
- Protection / Destruction
- Endurance / Weakness

Rory Briski

PERTHRO

Heimdall's Aett: 2-6
Element: WATER

RUNES for: *Divination (Basic)*

Conceptual Associations:
- *Well of Wyrd and Ability to Use its Power*
- Rune of Divination
- Rune of Meditation
- Good Luck
- Fellowship
- Happiness
- To Much of this Energy = Chaos, Destruction & Confusion

Keyword Associations:
- Good Luck / Addiction
- Joy / Loneliness
- Evolving / Stagnation

Rory Briski

ELHAZ

Heimdall's Aett: 2-7
Element: FIRE

RUNES for: *Divination (Basic)*

Conceptual Associations:

> *Communication Between Self and Higher-Self*
>
> Spiritual Growth
>
> Rune of Cleansing & Warding
>
> Used to Fare Through Worlds
>
> Divine Forces are at Play
>
> The Bifrost Bridge
>
> Divine Communication is Indicated – Be Wary

Keyword Associations:

> Connection with the Gods / Loss of Divine Link
>
> Protection / Hidden Danger

Rory Briski

SOWILO

Heimdall's Aett: 2-8
Element: NONE

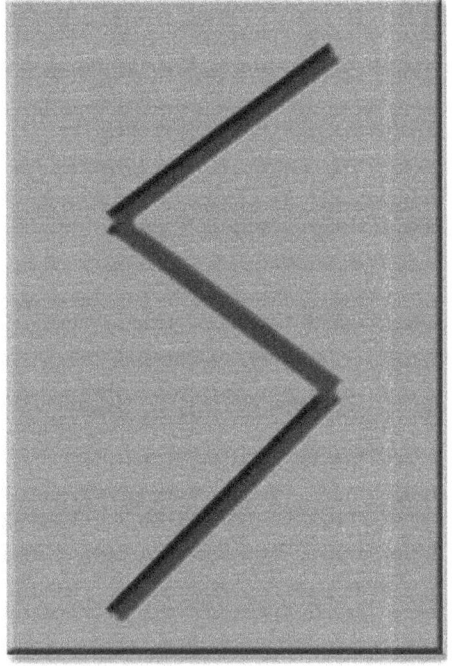

RUNES for: *Divination (Basic)*

Conceptual Associations:
> *Rune of Invincibility*
>
> Final Triumph
>
> Wheel of the Sun and Magical Will
>
> Invincible, Unstoppable Force
>
> Have Hope, Good Guidance is Being Given
>
> Fix on "Your" Goal for Success
>
> Honor & Luck
>
> Beware False Success by Dishonorable Means

Keyword Associations:
> Guidance / Gullibility
>
> Goals Achieved / False Goals
>
> Success / False Success

Tiwaz's Aett

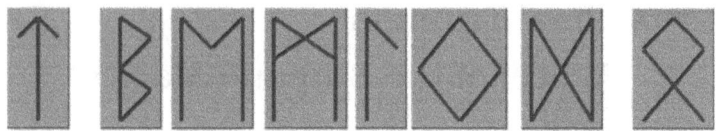

The third aett is called Tiwaz's aett. This aett is associated with the gods.

The energies of this aett are:

- ➢ The Sky-Father and victory (tiwaz)
- ➢ The great mother, birth and death (berkano)
- ➢ Twin Gods and Kings (ehwaz)
- ➢ The godly might of men and women (mannaz)
- ➢ The power of life and hidden resources (laguz)
- ➢ The god's sacrifice (ingwaz)
- ➢ Transcendent completion (dagaz)

RUNES for: *Divination (Basic)*

➢ The inheritance that encompasses all (othala)

Rory Briski

TIWAZ

Tiwaz's Aett: 3-1
Element: AIR

RUNES for: *Divination (Basic)*

Conceptual Associations:
- *Justice*
- Victory
- Letter of the Law
- Spiritual & Moral Strength
- Stability and Ordering Force
- Strength, Courage & Honor
- Victory if you Acted Wisely
- Beware Planning & Never Doing
- Success Through Self-Sacrifice
- Faith, Loyalty & Trust in the Face of Hardships
- Strive for Precision and Plan Carefully

Keyword Associations:
- Justice / Injustice
- Analysis / Paralysis
- Self-Sacrifice / Over-Sacrifice

Rory Briski

BERKANO

Tiwaz's Aett: 3-2
Element: EARTH

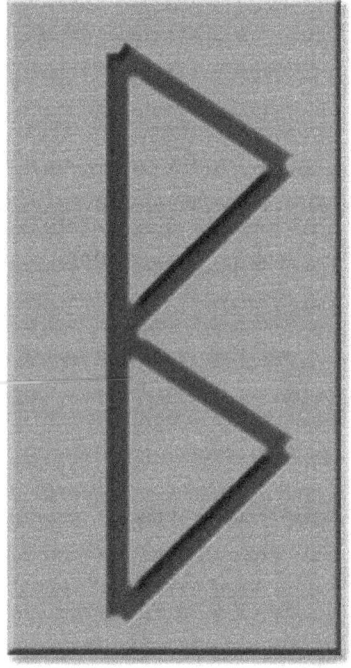

RUNES for: *Divination (Basic)*

Conceptual Associations:
- *Birth and Death*
- The Great Mother
- Bringing into Being
- New Beginnings & Gradual Changes
- New Aspects in Erotic Relationship
- Prosperity and Beauty
- Beware False Appearances
- Look for Importance in Small Things or New Things

Keyword Associations:
- Becoming / Stagnation
- Birth / Sterility
- Shelter / Deceit

Rory Briski

EHWAZ

Tiwaz's Aett: 3-3
Element: NONE

RUNES for: *Divination (Basic)*

Conceptual Associations:
- *Teamwork (Horse & Rider)(Sword & Scabbard)*
- Twin Gods & Kings
- Power Under Guidance of Wisdom
- Telepathic & Empathic Links
- Harmonious Union of Dualities
- Dynamic Harmony with Others
- Formal Partnership May Be Coming
- Accept Unique Differences
- Beware of Losing Self in Partner

Keyword Associations:
- Harmony / Disloyalty
- Loyalty / Betrayal
- Trust / Mistrust
- Teamwork / Duplication

Rory Briski

MANNAZ

Tiwaz's Aett: 3-4
Element: NONE

RUNES for: *Divination (Basic)*

Conceptual Associations:

Blinders Will Be Removed To See Things As They Are

Godly Might of Men and Women

Melds Reason and Intelligence

Strengthen Intelligence & Memory

Awaken and Guide Psychic Abilities

Happiness in Inner & Social Life

Don't Dwell on Mortality & Weakness

Beware Relationships Based on Lies and Misperceptions

Keyword Associations:

Awareness / Delusion

Intelligence / Blindness

Devine Structure / Mortality

Rory Briski

LAGUZ

Tiwaz's Aett: 3-5
Element: WATER

RUNES for: *Divination (Basic)*

Conceptual Associations:
> *Physical and Magical Strength and Insight*
>
> Do Not Fear the Journey
>
> Life Brought from Darkness
>
> Hidden Brought into the Light
>
> Power of Life & Hidden Sources
>
> Transition from One State of Being into Another
>
> Stern Tests in Life But You Have the Power to Overcome Them

Keyword Associations:
> Growth / Withering
>
> Vitality / Fear
>
> Journey / Circular Motion

Rory Briski

INGWAZ

Tiwaz's Aett: 3-6
Element: EARTH

RUNES for: *Divination (Basic)*

Conceptual Associations:
    Converts Active Energy into Potential Energy
    Have Patience
    Listen to Yourself
    Contained, Isolated Separation
    Rune by Which Power is Stored
    Active Internal Growth (Rest)
    This is a "Stage" not an "End"

Keyword Associations:
    Rest / Scattering
    Gestation / Impotence
    Internal Growth / Movement without Change

Rory Briski

DAGAZ

Tiwaz's Aett: 3-7
Element: NONE

RUNES for: *Divination (Basic)*

Conceptual Associations:
- *In the Light of Day All is Revealed*
- Meditation
- Achievement
- Transcendent Completion
- Enlightened Consciousness
- New Beginnings on a Higher Level
- Becoming One with the Universe
- A Great Awakening is at Hand
- Light Found Where You Don't Expect It
- Seek the Ideal

Keyword Associations:
- Awakening / Blindness
- Hope / Hopelessness
- Awareness / Deprivation

Rory Briski

OTHALA

Tiwaz's Aett: 3-8
Element: EARTH

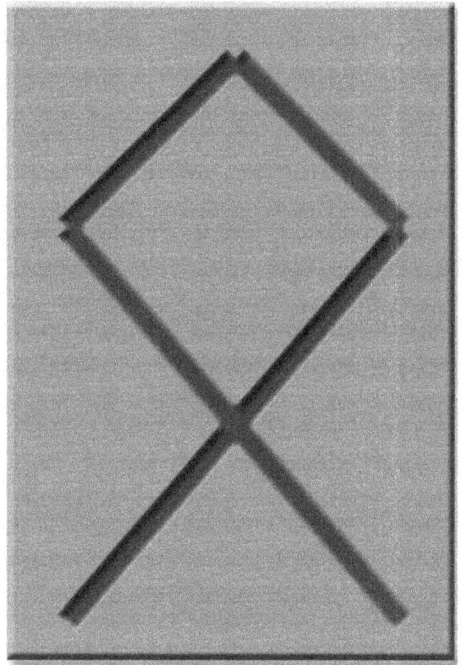

RUNES for: *Divination (Basic)*

Conceptual Associations:
> *Rune of Inheritance & Power from Ancestors and/or Past Lives*
>
> Inheritance That Encompasses All
>
> Wisdom & Power from Past Lives
>
> Strengthen the Ties of the Clan
>
> Stable Prosperity & Well Being
>
> Attention to Group/Clan Customs
>
> New Dwelling or Allegiance
>
> Wealth of Possessions & Immobile Property (Land)

Keyword Associations:
> Group Order / Totalitarianism
>
> Home / Homeless
>
> Group Prosperity / Poverty

Rory Briski

Rune Readings

There are several ways to conduct Rune readings and I will detail the two most basic methods here. These readings can easily be done using Runes with a variety of Rune shapes and sizes including ovals, rounds, squares, etc.

Runes can be carved into wood.

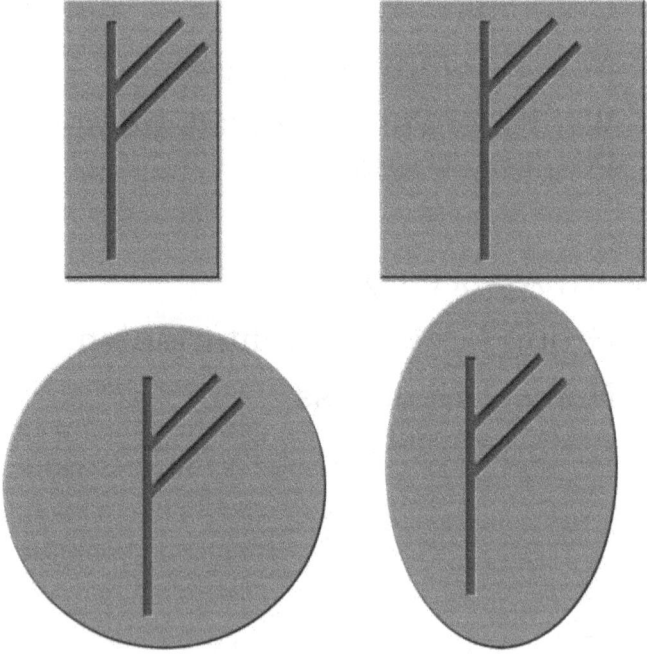

RUNES for: *Divination (Basic)*

Runes can also be carved into stone, molded into glass/plastic or stamped into metal.

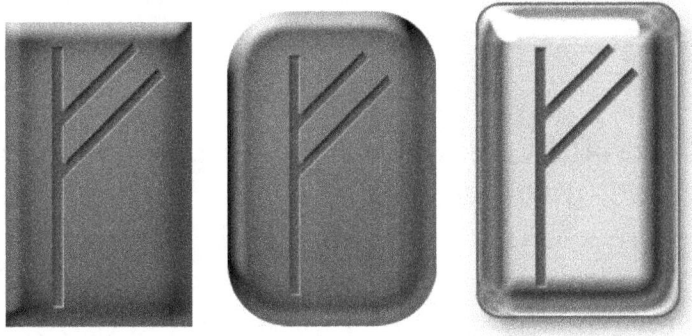

The Three Rune Spread

Place all of the runes into a bag and draw three Runes, one at a time. The order that the Runes are drawn from the bag is very important.

Alternately, you could dump all of the runes onto a table, turn them face down, shuffle them, and then pick three. Again, ensure to keep track of the order in which they are picked up.

Please note that there is no "reversed" meaning to the Runes. However, there are blockages and ways for some Runes to impact or impede others, but this is not typically determined from a simple drawing of a Rune upside-down.

RUNES for: *Divination (Basic)*

As the Runes are drawn, they each represent in turn:

➢ The first Rune (ruled by the Great Norn: Urdhr) indicates the past. All of the things in the questioners life leading up to this point, or the root of the problem.

➢ The second Rune (ruled by the Great Norn: Verhandi) indicates the forces acting on the question and happening now.

➢ The third Rune (ruled by the Great Norn: Skuld) indicates what will happen based on runes one and two if nothing else changes. Staying on present course, keeping doing what you are doing, etc.

Rory Briski

Example #1:

The person asks a question about finding a new job.

They reach into the bag of Runes and pull out one rune at a time. The Runes drawn are:

Rune	Name	Aett Position
1st	Elhaz	(2-7)

RUNES for: *Divination (Basic)*

Rune	Name	Aett Position
2nd	Laguz	(3-5)

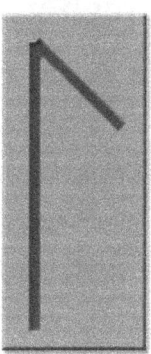

Rune	Name	Aett Position
3rd	Wunjo	(1-8)

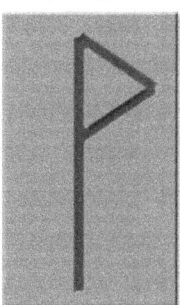

Rory Briski

The Past: Elhaz indicates that divine forces have been at work or that the questioners higher-self has been influencing the situation.

The Present: Laguz indicates the person is currently going through tough times and tests but has the inner strength to overcome them.

A Possible Future: Wunjo indicates social and domestic harmony with new business relationships resulting in prosperity. Organization is also called for.

My Interpretation: I take this to mean that if the seeker gets organized they will find a new and prosperous opportunity.

Additionally, an equal number of Runes from each aett was drawn, one Rune each in this case, does not indicate any special attention needs to be put on any aett as a whole.

RUNES for: *Divination (Basic)*

For example, if all three Runes came from the first aett, then that may indicate a strong influence of the basic and primal forces within the seeker. Alternately, it could mean the raw abilities within the seeker. It all depends on the question and circumstances surrounding that particular question.

Rory Briski

Example #2:

Assume that the seeker had asked a different question, but the same Runes were drawn as in Example #1.

The person asks a question about their health.

They reach into the bag of Runes and pull out one rune at a time. The Runes drawn are:

Rune	Name	Aett Position
1st	Elhaz	(2-7)
2nd	Laguz	(3-5)
3rd	Wunjo	(1-8)

RUNES for: *Divination (Basic)*

The Past: Elhaz indicates that Spiritual Growth and Cleansing have been taking place.

The Present: Laguz indicates the person is going through a transition from one state into another.

A Possible Future: Wunjo indicates physical and emotional healing and harmony.

My Interpretation: I take this to mean that the seeker has been on a path of transformation and it is manifesting itself physically, giving rise to some uncomfortable issues.

However, at the end of the day, if the transformation continues, the seeker will have physical and emotional harmony.

Rory Briski

The Nine Rune Spread

This is similar to the three Rune spread except that three runes are drawn for each of the time phases. That is, three for past, three for present and three for possible future.

Each group of three Runes drawn is then read for each time phase.

This gives a more comprehensive reading about the basis of the situation and possible outcomes.

You may put the Runes back into the bag for each set of three draws. As previously mentioned, in rune casting, it is believed that the three Great Norns (Fates) help guide which runes are drawn for each grouping.

RUNES for: *Divination (Basic)*

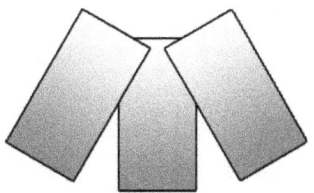

The Past

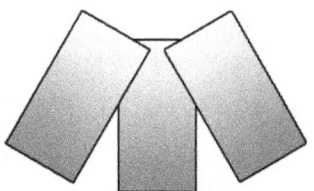

The Present

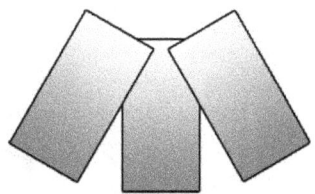

The Future

Rory Briski

Runic Interrelationships

Interrelationships between the Runes can be more clearly seen when you look at the three aettir as a 3 by 8 matrix.

As previously mentioned, during the reading you want to watch for patterns to develop as to which aett the runes belong to, and which position within the aett they belong.

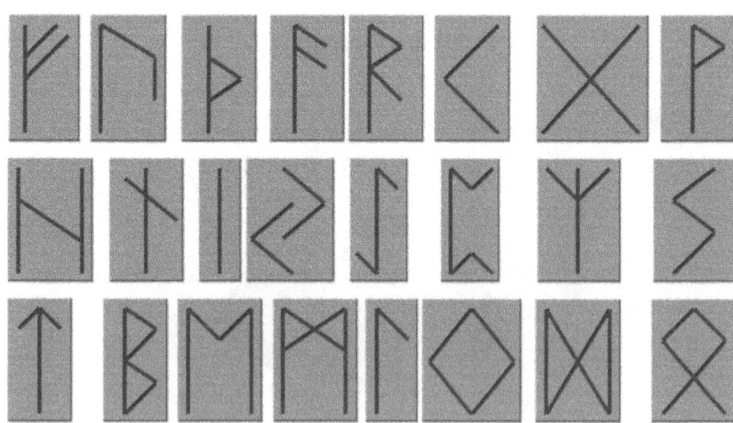

RUNES for: *Divination (Basic)*

Look for a predominance of runes from a single aett, or from different aettir positioned within the beginning, middle or end of the aett.

Runes drawn from similar positions within the aettir show a special interrelationship and significance to each other.

Rune Tines

I'll briefly mention Rune Tines here but these will be detailed more fully in another book, "RUNES for: *Divination* (Advanced)".

Rune Tines are Runes that have been carved onto elongated sticks. These can then be used in more complex Rune readings and divination practices. Here is where the concept of a Rune showing up in a reading as more helpful or less helpful comes from. Not necessarily as "reversed" but in how it positively or negatively impacts other Runes in the reading.

For example, you could have ISA crossing FEHU, which could indicate a stagnation or blockage in money matters. Other Runes and their relation to each other would tell more of the story. All 24 Runes are used in these types of readings.

RUNES for: *Divination (Basic)*

It is highly recommended that you become comfortable with the divination practices of the basic 3 and/or 9 Rune spreads before attempting divinations with Rune Tines.

An example of Rune Tines:

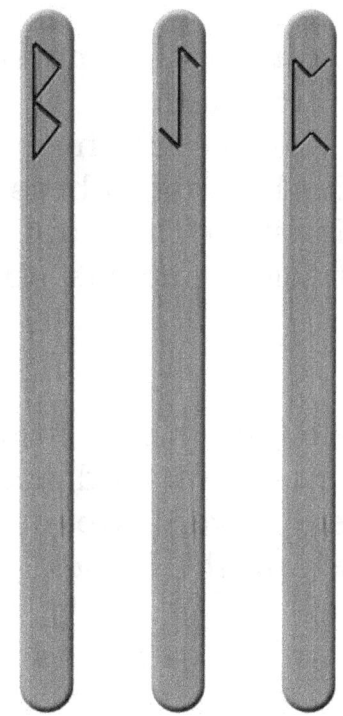

Rory Briski

Runes, Tarot & Astrology

While there is no historical evidence to support the old Norse or Teutonics believed in or practiced Tarot or Astrology, there has been some discussions over the past few decades about the Runes and how they relate to these other forms of divination.

It is possible to find some similarities in these other methods of divination and to the Runes, but these are really just aids in helping others that are more familiar with Tarot and Astrology get some "basic" concepts about using the Runes.

Just as there are many nuances and complexities in Tarot and Astrology, so to are there layers upon layers of meanings within the Runes.

RUNES for: *Divination (Basic)*

	Rune	Tarot	Astrology
1	Fehu	Empress	Aries
2	Uruz	Chariot	Taurus
3	Thurisaz	Emperor	Mars
4	Ansuz	Hierophant	Jupiter
5	Raidho	Chariot	Sagittarius
6	Kenaz	Hermit	Venus
7	Gebo	Lovers	Libra
8	Wunjo	Sun	Pisces / Aquarius
9	Hagalaz	Tower	Uranus
10	Nauthiz	Chariot	Capricorn
11	Isa	Hanged Man	Moon
12	Jera	Wheel of Fortune	Venus / Libra
13	Eihwaz	Death	Scorpio
14	Perthro	Wheel of Fortune	Jupiter
15	Elhaz	High Priestess	Saturn
16	Sowilo	Sun	Sun

Rory Briski

	Rune	**Tarot**	**Astrology**
17	Tiwaz	Justice	Libra / Virgo
18	Berkano	Empress	Virgo / Venus
19	Ehwaz	Lovers	Gemini
20	Mannaz	Magician	Jupiter
21	Laguz	Moon	Moon
22	Ingwaz	Temperance	Moon / Cancer
23	Dagaz	Judgment	Moon / Pisces / Neptune
24	Othala	Moon	Moon

RUNES for: *Divination (Basic)*

Thank You

Thank you for taking some of your valuable time and sharing it with me. I trust that this book has helped you to explore your curiosity about the Runes and I encourage you to delve further into their mysteries.

Please look for additional books in the "RUNES for:" series.

The author may be contacted via www.SpiralJourney.com.

www.ingramcontent.com/pod-product-compliance
Lightning Source LLC
Chambersburg PA
CBHW071724040426
42446CB00011B/2204